GRAPHIC BIOGRAPHIES

CLARA BARTON

Angel of the Battlefield

by Allison Lassieur

illustrated by Brian Bascle

Consultants:

The Staff of the Clara Barton National Historic Site

Glen Echo, Maryland

Capstone
press

Graphic Library is published by Capstone Press,
151 Good Counsel Drive, P.O. Box 669, Mankato, Minnesota 56002.
www.capstonepress.com

1 2 3 4 5 6 10 09 08 07 06 05

Library of Congress Cataloging-in-Publication Data
Lassieur, Allison.
Clara Barton: angel of the battlefield/by Allison Lassieur; illustrated by Brian Bascle.
    p. cm.—(Graphic library. Graphic biographies)
    Includes bibliographical references and index.
    ISBN 0–7368–4632–8 (hardcover)
    ISBN 0–7368–6192-0 (softcover)
    1. Barton, Clara, 1821–1912—Juvenile literature. 2. Nurses—United States—Biography—
Juvenile literature. I. Bascle, Brian. II. Title. III. Series.
HV569.B3L37 2006
361.7'634'092—dc22   2005008122

Summary: In graphic novel format, tells the life story of Clara Barton, who served as a Civil War
nurse and started the American Red Cross.

Art and Editorial Direction
Jason Knudson and Blake A. Hoena

Designers
Jason Knudson and Jennifer Bergstrom

Editor
Rebecca Glaser

Editor's note: Direct quotations from primary sources are indicated by a yellow background.

Direct quotations appear on the following pages:
Page 8, letter from Stephen Barton Jr. to Clara Barton, July 1851; Page 9, letter from Clara Barton
    to Bernard Vassall, 1851; Pages 15, 16, letter from Dr. James Dunn, army surgeon, to his
    wife; Page 26, letter from Clara Barton to Halsted, April 1906; all quoted in *Clara Barton:
    Professional Angel* by Elizabeth Brown Pryor (Philadelphia: University of Pennsylvania
    Press, 1987).
Page 11, letter from Clara Barton to Bernard Vassall; page 13, letter from Clara Barton to ladies in
    Worchester; Page 17, journal entry; all quoted in *Clara Barton National Historic Site
    Handbook* by National Park Service (Washington, D.C.: Division of Publications, 1981).
Page 19, Clara Barton's war lecture, Library of Congress papers, http://memory.loc.gov/
    cgi-bin/ampage
Page 24, editorial from the Johnstown Daily Tribune, quoted in *The Red Cross in Peace and War*
    by Clara Barton (Washington, D.C.: American Historical Press, 1899).
Page 27, quoted in *The Life of Clara Barton* by Percy H. Epler. (New York: The Macmillian
    Company, 1915).

TABLE OF CONTENTS

Chapter 1
THE MAKING OF A HEROINE

Clara Barton was born on December 25, 1821, in the small town of North Oxford, Massachusetts. As she grew up, her older brothers and sisters taught her many things.

Stack the blocks this way, Clara.

Here, let me show you.

It's close to your bedtime, Clara.

Clara's brothers and sisters were more than 10 years older than she was. Later in life, Clara said that she "had no playmates, but in effect six fathers and mothers."

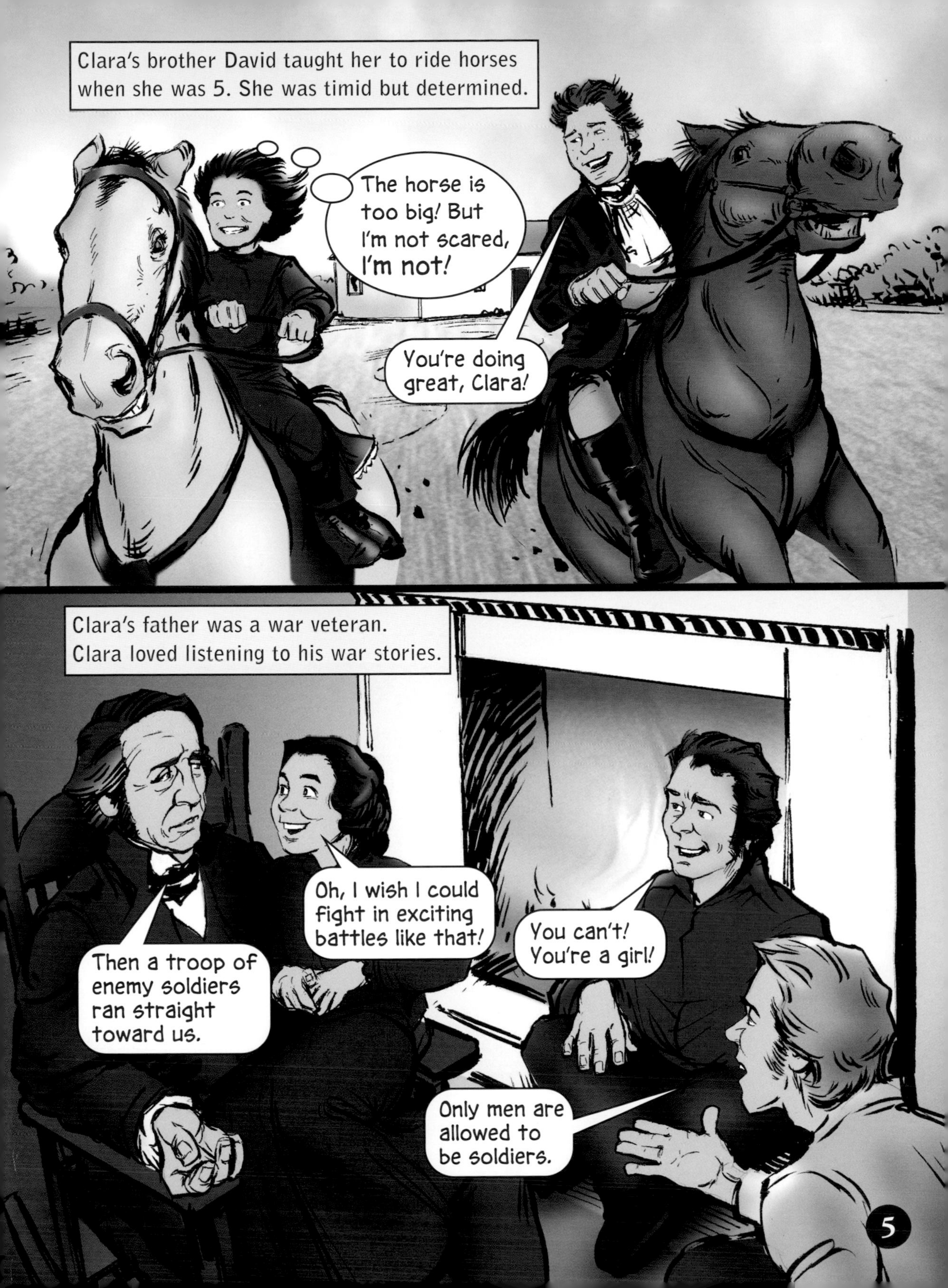
Clara's brother David taught her to ride horses when she was 5. She was timid but determined.
The horse is too big! But I'm not scared, I'm not!
You're doing great, Clara!
Clara's father was a war veteran. Clara loved listening to his war stories.
Then a troop of enemy soldiers ran straight toward us.
Oh, I wish I could fight in exciting battles like that!
You can't! You're a girl!
Only men are allowed to be soldiers.

When Clara was 12 years old, her brother David fell from a rafter while building a barn roof. He was hurt badly, and he suffered from headaches and fever.

Here, David, take this medicine and you'll feel better.

During the two years while David was sick, Clara only left his bedside for a half day.

Clara, you've been an angel these last two years.

I was glad to help. It gave me something useful to do.

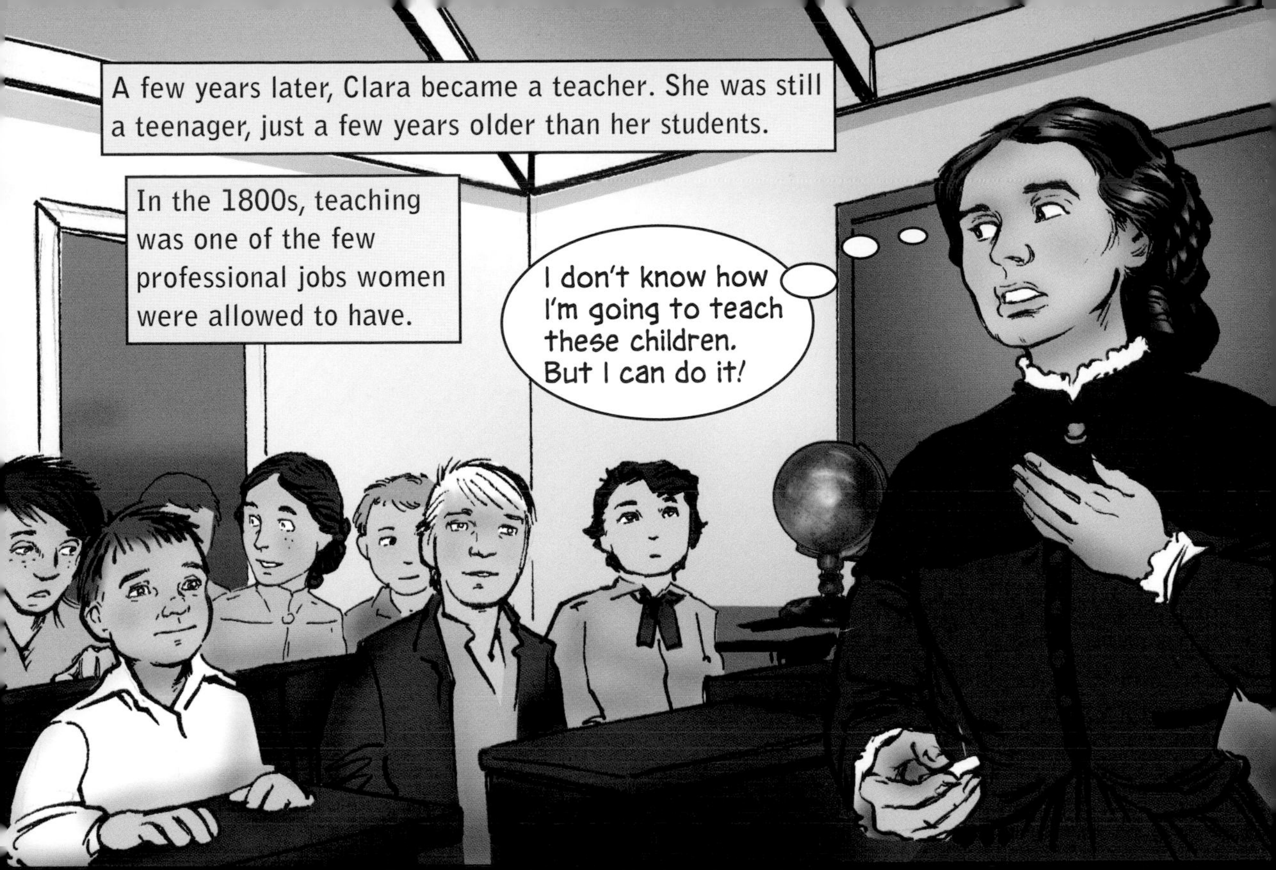
A few years later, Clara became a teacher. She was still a teenager, just a few years older than her students.
In the 1800s, teaching was one of the few professional jobs women were allowed to have.
I don't know how I'm going to teach these children. But I can do it!

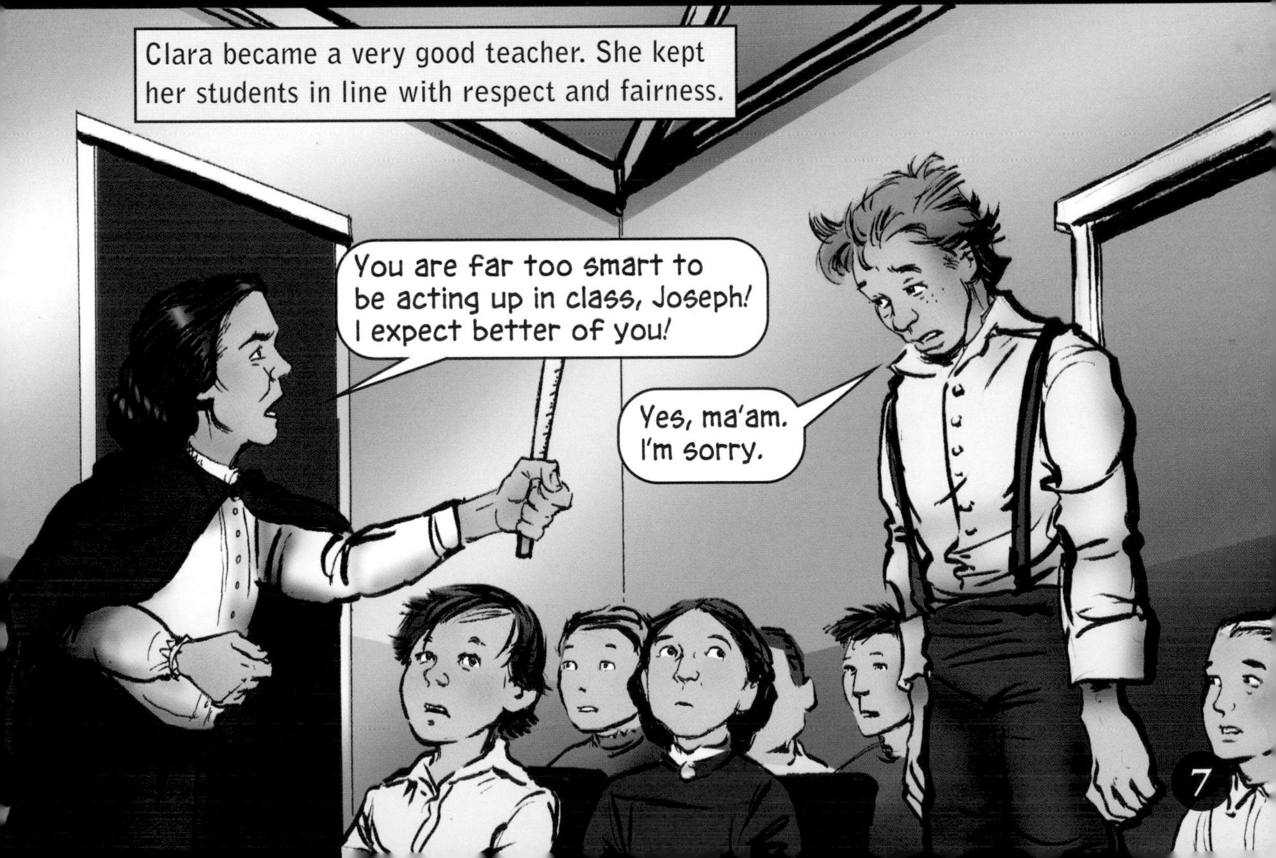
Clara became a very good teacher. She kept her students in line with respect and fairness.
You are far too smart to be acting up in class, Joseph! I expect better of you!
Yes, ma'am. I'm sorry.

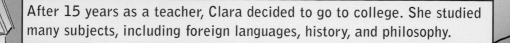

After 15 years as a teacher, Clara decided to go to college. She studied many subjects, including foreign languages, history, and philosophy.

Clara, you are taking more classes than any other student.

I want to learn as much as I can.

While Clara was at college, she received sad news from her brother Stephen.

July 1851

Our excellent mother is no more. She died this afternoon at a quarter after five o'clock. Her last end was without a struggle and apparently easy.

~Stephen

I wish I weren't so far from home!

Clara had received the news of her mother's death too late to go to the funeral. She returned home at the end of the term.

I have nowhere to go, no one to go to, nothing to go with, and no way of earning my living if I did go anywhere.

Back home with no job and nothing to challenge her, she wasn't sure what to do next.

After a few months at home, Clara decided it was time to try something new.

I'm glad my friends invited me to live with them in New Jersey.

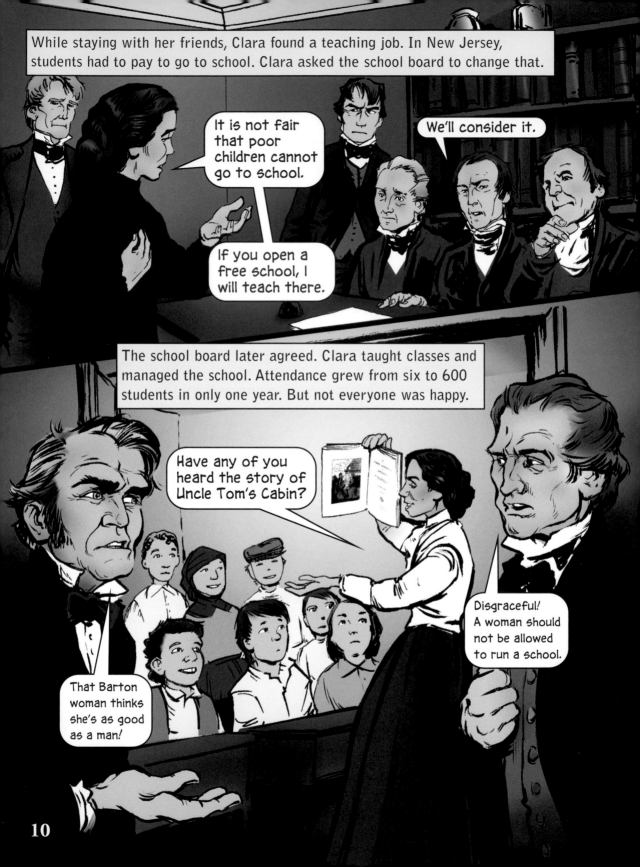

While staying with her friends, Clara found a teaching job. In New Jersey, students had to pay to go to school. Clara asked the school board to change that.

It is not fair that poor children cannot go to school.

We'll consider it.

If you open a free school, I will teach there.

The school board later agreed. Clara taught classes and managed the school. Attendance grew from six to 600 students in only one year. But not everyone was happy.

Have any of you heard the story of Uncle Tom's Cabin?

Disgraceful! A woman should not be allowed to run a school.

That Barton woman thinks she's as good as a man!

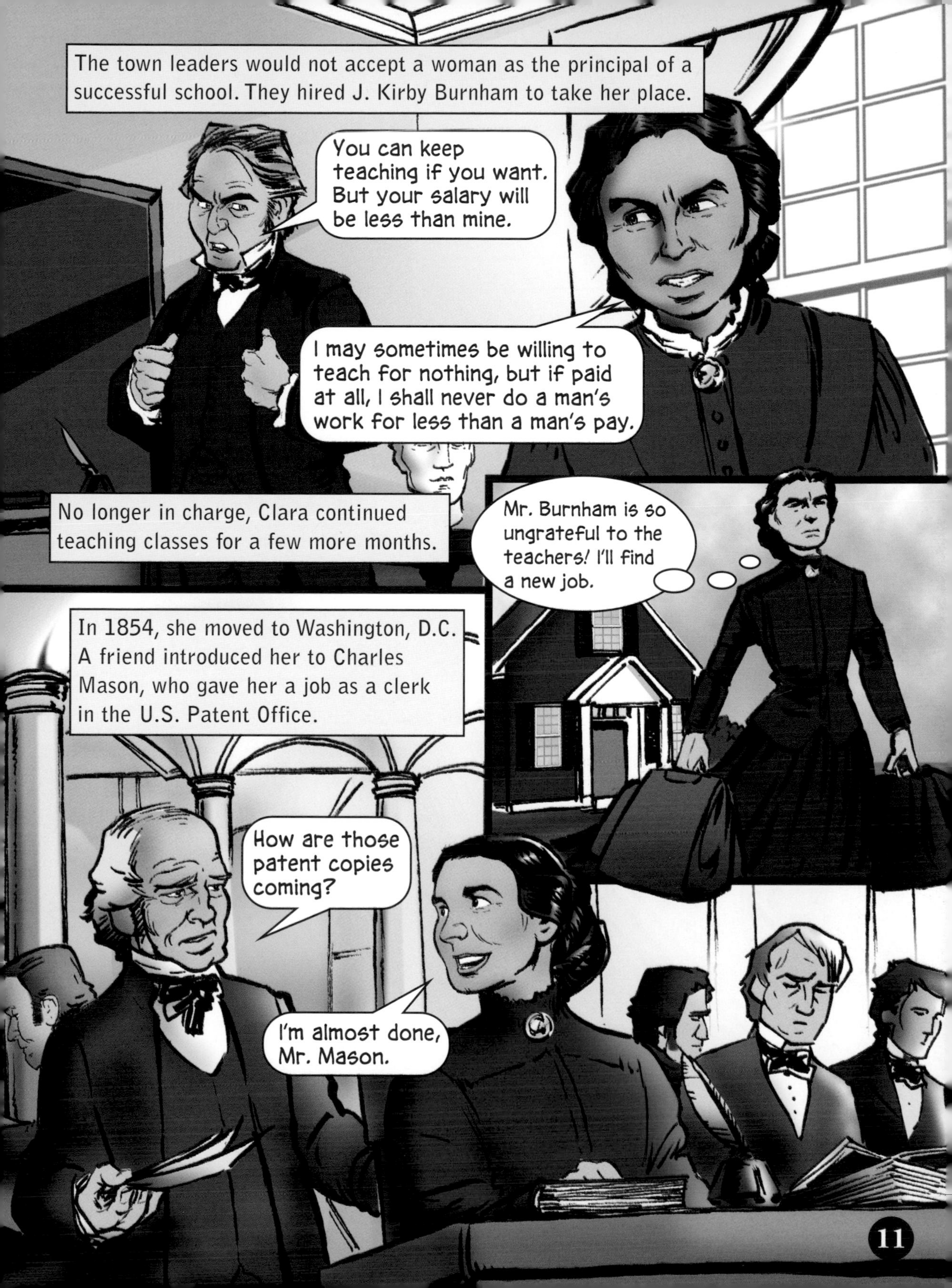

The town leaders would not accept a woman as the principal of a successful school. They hired J. Kirby Burnham to take her place.
You can keep teaching if you want. But your salary will be less than mine.
I may sometimes be willing to teach for nothing, but if paid at all, I shall never do a man's work for less than a man's pay.
No longer in charge, Clara continued teaching classes for a few more months.
Mr. Burnham is so ungrateful to the teachers! I'll find a new job.
In 1854, she moved to Washington, D.C. A friend introduced her to Charles Mason, who gave her a job as a clerk in the U.S. Patent Office.
How are those patent copies coming?
I'm almost done, Mr. Mason.

Chapter 2
THE CIVIL WAR

For years, northern states and southern states had argued over slavery and other issues. The southern states broke away from the U.S. and formed their own country. But the North wanted to save the Union. By April 1861, the Civil War had begun.

Washington, D.C., became a hub for the North's army. Clara, like many others, greeted the arriving soldiers. One day, she spotted boys from her hometown.

Remember me, Miss Barton? You were my teacher.

How are you, Joseph? Does the army treat you well?

We don't have enough soap, bandages . . .

We don't get much food either.

TRAIN DEPOT

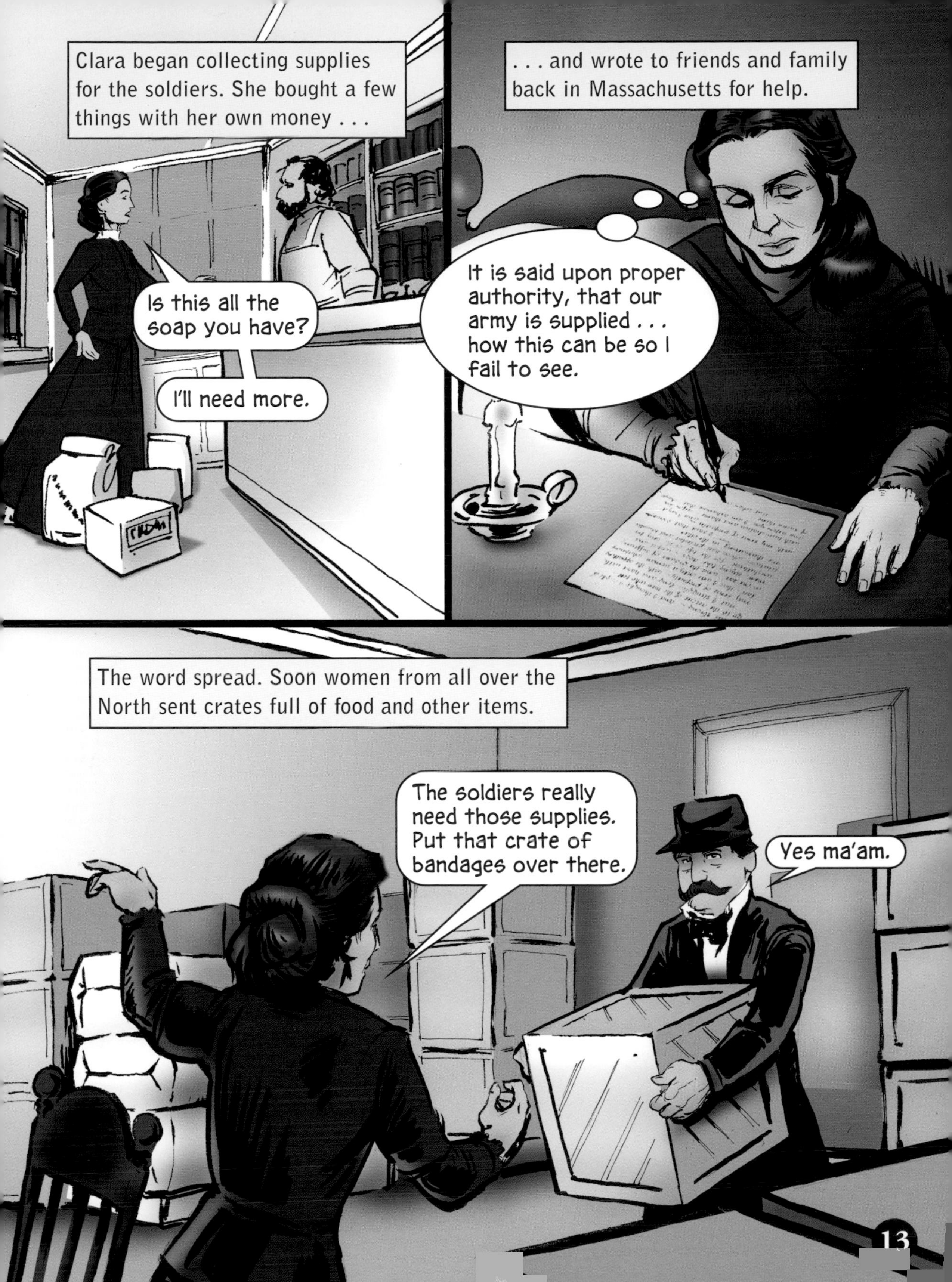
Clara began collecting supplies for the soldiers. She bought a few things with her own money . . .
Is this all the soap you have?
I'll need more.
. . . and wrote to friends and family back in Massachusetts for help.
It is said upon proper authority, that our army is supplied . . . how this can be so I fail to see.
The word spread. Soon women from all over the North sent crates full of food and other items.
The soldiers really need those supplies. Put that crate of bandages over there.
Yes ma'am.

Clara soon became a welcome face to the tired, hungry, and injured soldiers.

I've got honey and lemons.

Thank you, ma'am.

And fresh bandages.

You're an angel.

By the time injured soldiers arrived in Washington, they were in bad shape. Clara knew she could do more if she helped them soon after they were hurt. She asked Colonel Rucker to let her take medical supplies to army hospitals near battlefields.

I want to go to the front to help the soldiers.

The front is no place for a lady!

I have three warehouses full of bandages and food!

Well, the men could certainly use them. I'll give you permission.

Army hospitals were dirty and low on supplies. Clara and an assistant set to work cleaning, cooking fresh food, and handing out medical supplies.

With Clara's extra supplies and help, the hospital conditions improved. Army doctors praised her work.

The army wasn't prepared to take care of all these wounded soldiers. Thank goodness for Miss Barton.

At a time when we were entirely out of dressings of every kind, she supplied us with everything.

If heaven ever sent out an angel, she must be one.

Clara spent the rest of the war caring for the soldiers. Through it all, her only thought was to be useful to the men who needed her help.

Dearest wife,
. . . We had nothing but our instruments . . . When the railroad cars whistled up to the station, the first person on the platform was Miss Barton again to supply us with bandages and every article that could be thought of . . .
                    Your husband,
              Dr. James Dunn, army surgeon

MISS BARTON NEARLY SHOT
In the battle of Antietam, Miss Barton narrowly missed death when a bullet ripped through her sleeve, killing the soldier she was nursing.

MISS BARTON CALM DURING DANGEROUS BATTLE
At the battle of Fredericksburg, Miss Barton calmly tended the wounded even when the room she was in was attacked by enemy fire.

august 1

My work and words are bound up in the individual soldier — what he does, sees, feels, or thinks, in long dread hours of leaden rain and iron hail.

Chapter 3
One War Ends, Another Begins

The North won the Civil War in 1865. But Clara's work didn't end there. She helped families find missing soldiers.

Any news of my brother, Frank Adams?

He was taken prisoner in 1864. He's still in Georgia.

I'm so glad he's alive! Thank you!

The following year, Clara began traveling and speaking about her war experiences.

. . . And among the trees were laid the wounded, who were pouring in by scores of wagon loads.

All day they came— and the whole hill was covered.

When her two-year-long speaking tour was done, Clara began feeling useless and ignored. She again became depressed. Her doctor thought a trip to Europe would be good for her health. She agreed to go.

Good-bye!

Have a good time!

I'll miss you!

In 1870, while Clara was in Europe, France declared war on the country of Prussia and its German allies. During the Franco-Prussian War, a group called the International Red Cross helped wounded soldiers and their families.

Our group serves anyone in need.

I'll help in any way I can.

I wish we'd had a group like this during the Civil War.

Clara made herself a Red Cross armband and went to work.

She handed out supplies to families in France and Germany whose homes had been destroyed by war.

Merci, merci.

You're welcome.

After the war ended and Clara's relief work was done, she visited other places in Europe. England was her last stop. With nothing to do, she became bored. Depression and sickness came over her again.

I feel like I'm wasting my life. I need to do something useful.

Even a visit from her friend the Grand Duchess of Germany could not cheer her up.

I present you the Iron Cross of Germany for your help in our hospitals.

Thank you.

When Clara got news that her sister Sally was sick with cancer, she sailed back home.

Chapter 4
THE RED CROSS

Clara returned to the United States in 1873. Depressed and ill after Sally's death, she took time to rest and recover. When she felt better, she began to think about starting a Red Cross group in the United States.

But we don't need the Red Cross. There will never be another war here.

The Red Cross could also help victims of natural disasters like floods and hurricanes.

Clara had a big job ahead of her. Few Americans had heard of the Red Cross. For several years she gave lectures . . .

. . . wrote letters to Congressmen . . .

The United States is the *only* civilized nation that has not joined the Red Cross.

. . . and gave out pamphlets about the Red Cross to anyone who would take them.

THE RED CROSS

In the middle of a war or a natural disaster, people need help right away. The Red Cross will organize instant relief.

All her work paid off. On May 12, 1881, Clara and a group of supporters founded the American Red Cross.

I can't keep doing this alone. Will you help me?

Yes!

We will help you. America needs the Red Cross.

Over the next two decades, the Red Cross aided victims of disasters around the country.

In 1884, Red Cross workers brought supplies to flood victims along the Ohio and Mississippi rivers.

In 1889, Clara and the Red Cross spent five months helping flood victims in Johnstown, Pennsylvania.

Johnstown Daily Tribune

October 23, 1889

FAREWELL TO MISS BARTON

How shall we thank Miss Clara Barton and the Red Cross for the help they have given us? We cannot thank Miss Barton in words. Hunt the dictionaries of all languages through and you will not find the signs to express our appreciation of her and her work. Try to describe the sunshine, try to describe the starlight. Words fail.

In 1893, a hurricane pounded the South Carolina coast. The Red Cross delivered food and helped people re-plant crops in ruined fields.

In 1900, a hurricane in Galveston, Texas, left 6,000 people homeless. Clara took a group of Red Cross workers to help. She was 78 years old.

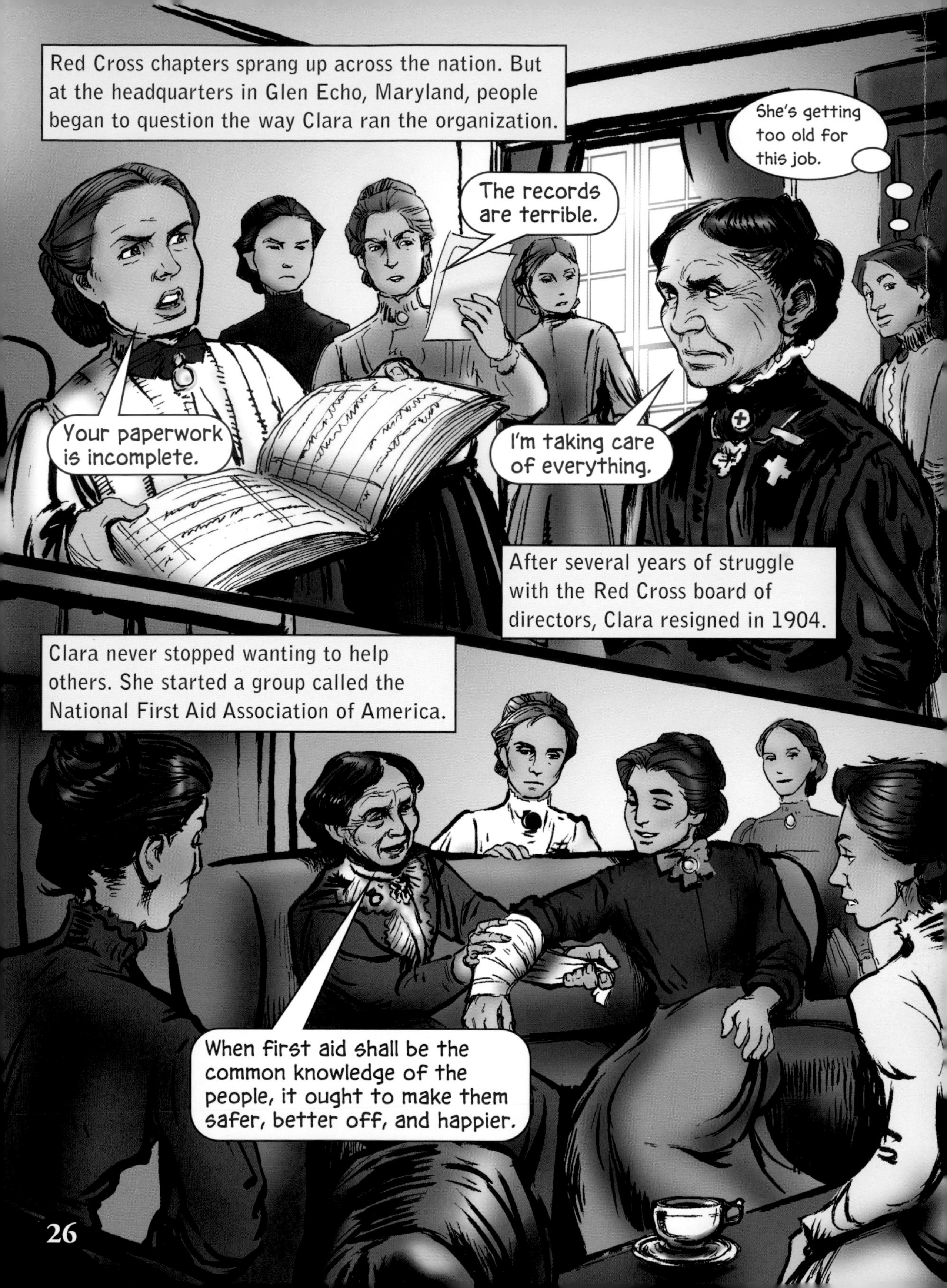
Red Cross chapters sprang up across the nation. But at the headquarters in Glen Echo, Maryland, people began to question the way Clara ran the organization.
Your paperwork is incomplete.
The records are terrible.
She's getting too old for this job.
I'm taking care of everything.
After several years of struggle with the Red Cross board of directors, Clara resigned in 1904.
Clara never stopped wanting to help others. She started a group called the National First Aid Association of America.
When first aid shall be the common knowledge of the people, it ought to make them safer, better off, and happier.

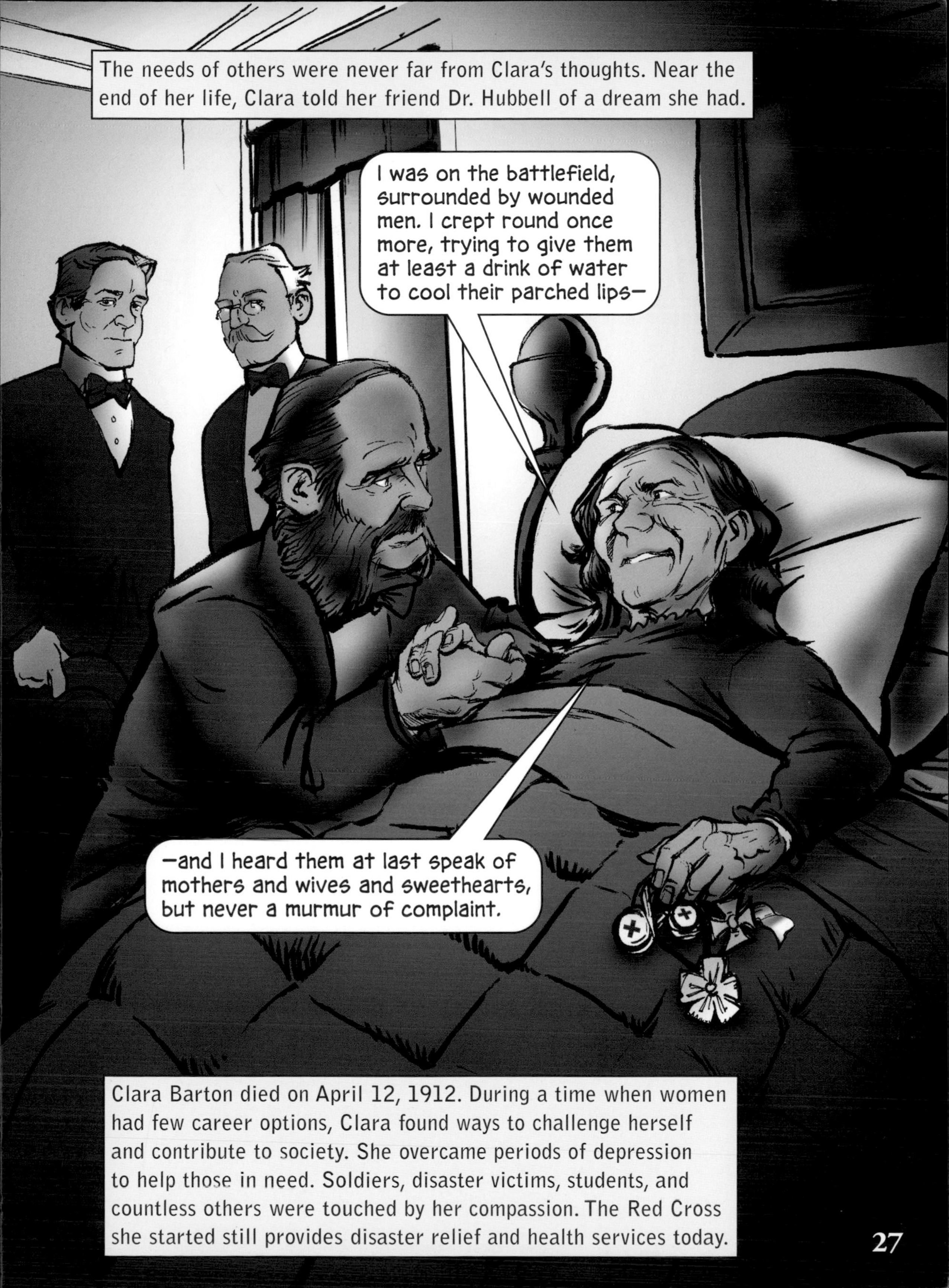
The needs of others were never far from Clara's thoughts. Near the end of her life, Clara told her friend Dr. Hubbell of a dream she had.
I was on the battlefield, surrounded by wounded men. I crept round once more, trying to give them at least a drink of water to cool their parched lips—
—and I heard them at last speak of mothers and wives and sweethearts, but never a murmur of complaint.
Clara Barton died on April 12, 1912. During a time when women had few career options, Clara found ways to challenge herself and contribute to society. She overcame periods of depression to help those in need. Soldiers, disaster victims, students, and countless others were touched by her compassion. The Red Cross she started still provides disaster relief and health services today.

More about CLARA BARTON

✚ Clarissa Harlowe Barton was born on Christmas Day—December 25, 1821.

✚ Although Clara supported the North during the Civil War, her compassion reached everyone. She nursed soldiers from both the North and the South.

✚ Clara never mended the hole in her sleeve after the battle of Antietam. She said, "I wonder if a soldier ever does mend a bullet hole in his coat?"

✚ After the Civil War, Clara helped find 22,000 missing soldiers. She advertised in newspapers and post offices, asking people to send her information. As letters came in, she notified soldiers' families.

✚ Clara met women's rights leader Susan B. Anthony and supported the campaign for women's right to vote. Clara also supported allowing black men to vote.

✚ The International Red Cross was founded in Geneva, Switzerland. Countries that joined the organization agreed not to attack doctors, nurses, or injured soldiers. Army medical units would display a red cross so they would be safe during war.

- Barton County, Kansas, was named for Clara. It is the only county in Kansas named after a woman.

- Clara wrote several books, including *The Story of My Childhood* and *The Red Cross in Peace and War*.

- Before she moved in, Clara's house in Glen Echo, Maryland, was used as a warehouse for the Red Cross.

- Clara died on April 12, 1912, at her Glen Echo home. Her home is now a National Historic Site.

GLOSSARY

clerk (KLURK)—a person who copies and keeps track of records

depression (di-PRESH-uhn)—a condition of deep sadness and hopelessness

dressing (DRESS-ing)—a covering or bandage for a wound

pamphlet (PAM-flit)—a small, thin booklet that contains information about one topic

patent (PAT-uhnt)—a legal document giving an inventor the sole rights to make or sell his or her invention

score (SKOR)—a group of twenty things

timid (TIM-id)—shy and fearful

veteran (VET-ur-uhn)—a person who has served in the armed forces, especially during a war

INTERNET SITES

FactHound offers a safe, fun way to find Internet sites related to this book. All of the sites on FactHound have been researched by our staff.

Here's how:

1. Visit *www.facthound.com*
2. Type in this special code **0736846328** for age-appropriate sites. Or enter a search word related to this book for a more general search.
3. Click on the **Fetch It** button.

FactHound will fetch the best sites for you!